MATH ALL AROUND!

The Math of **Everyday Life**

Written by Anne Rooney

www.worldbook.com

Co-published by agreement between Shi Tu Hui and World Book, Inc.

Shi Tu Hui
Room 1807, Block 1,
#3 West Dawang Road
Chaoyang District, Beijing 100025
P.R. China

World Book, Inc.
180 North LaSalle Street
Suite 900
Chicago, Illinois 60601
USA

© 2026. All rights reserved. This volume may not be reproduced in whole or in part in any form without prior written permission from the publisher.

WORLD BOOK and the GLOBE DEVICE are registered trademarks or trademarks of World Book, Inc.

Library of Congress Control Number: 2025942098

Aha! Academy: Math
ISBN: 978-0-7166-7377-4 (set, hardcover)

Math All Around! The Math of Everyday Life
ISBN: 978-0-7166-7379-8 (hard cover)
ISBN: 978-0-7166-7442-9 (e-book)
ISBN: 978-0-7166-7432-0 (soft cover)

Staff

Editorial

Vice President
Tom Evans

Editorial Project Coordinator
Kaile Kilner

Senior Curriculum Designer
Caroline Davidson

Curriculum Designer
Mikayla Kightlinger

Proofreader
Nathalie Strassheim

Indexer
Nathaniel Lindstrom

Graphics and Design

Senior Visual
Communications Designer
Melanie Bender

Designer
Shannon Hagman

Written by Anne Rooney

Acknowledgments

The publishers gratefully acknowledge the following sources for photography. All illustrations were prepared by WORLD BOOK unless otherwise noted.

Cover: Eric Isselee/Shutterstock; Konstantin Zibert/Shutterstock; leungchopan/Shutterstock; Sergii Kumer/Shutterstock; Sergey_Bogomyako/Shutterstock

Saifstock/Adobe Stock 16; © ADDICTIVE STOCK CREATIVES/Alamy 26; © Aflo Co. Ltd./Alamy 11; © Westend61 GmbH/Alamy 37; NASA 25, 29; © Shutterstock 4, 5, 6, 7, 8, 9, 10, 11, 12, 13, 14, 15, 16, 17, 18, 19, 20, 21, 22, 23, 24, 25, 26, 27, 28, 29, 31, 35, 36, 37, 38, 39, 40, 41, 42, 43, 44, 46, 47, 48

There is a glossary of terms on page 48. Terms defined in the glossary are in type that looks like *this* on their first appearance on any spread (two facing pages).

Contents

Introduction 4
① **Measuring up** 6
    Divide and rule 8
    Near enough 10
    Quick change 12
② **All areas** 14
    Flat out 16
    Re-do your room .18
    More pizza? 20
③ **In proportion** 22
    All the same 24
    Lemonade stand. .26
    Plots and plans 28
④ **Save or spend?** 30
    Buy, buy, buy 32
    One in a hundred 34
    A lot of interest 36
⑤ **In the center** 38
    Know what to expect 40
    On trend 42
Activity 44
Index 46
Glossary 48

Introduction

Math isn't just for school—you use math all day, every day, without thinking about it! From making a cake, through saving for a treat, to detangling your hair, there's math all around you. Often, you use it without even realizing.

Being aware of the math around you can improve your life. Is a larger pizza better value than a smaller one? How much better? Did your teacher calculate your score correctly? Can you rearrange your room? How much paint will you need? Let's take a look at some of the places math is lurking in everyday life.

Math doesn't have to hurt!

Math helps you untangle your hair! Start near the ends, otherwise tangles become tighter as you squash them—increasing what mathematicians call "link density."

1 MEASURING UP

Measurements are all around you: the weight marked on your breakfast cereal, your clothes labeled with their size, and road signs telling you the distance to your destination. We have different **units** of measurement for different things, and have to pick the right kind. You can't weigh your puppy in minutes or say how long a movie is in inches!

The length of a bus journey is measured in minutes.

Milk is measured in pints.

The weight of a dog is measured in pounds or kilograms.

Some things have their own special units of measurement: the height of a horse can be measured in *hands*.

How much, how heavy, how long, how fast...? All these questions need us to measure something.

You don't only need to use the right kind of unit. You also need to pick the right scale for the size of item you are measuring. We don't weigh a hamburger in tons or buy ribbon by the mile. We have lots of different kinds of units and sometimes need to convert between them, which takes a bit more math.

Tiny germs are measured in *nanometers* (1 nm = 0.00000004 inches!).

Read on to discover how measurements show up every day and how you can use them successfully.

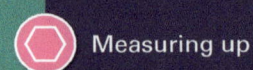
Measuring up

Divide and rule

Suppose you're 4 feet 9 inches tall. That's nice and clear. You could say you are 4 ¾ feet tall, or 57 inches tall, but you probably wouldn't, even though they mean the same. People would have to think about "57 inches" to realize you're a bit under 5 feet tall. Although "4 ¾ feet" works this time, "4 ¹¹⁄₁₂ feet" doesn't work well.

Yards and miles are also used to measure height and length. But you probably wouldn't say you were 1.583 yards tall, and you certainly wouldn't say you were 0.0009 miles tall! At the other end of the scale, you wouldn't give the distance to your school in inches.

All these children are 0.0009 miles tall—which is why we don't measure their height in miles!

When someone asks how tall you are, you probably give a number of feet and inches. These are two *units* we use to measure height or length. We have other units to measure weight, *volume*, time, and a host of other things.

This is why we have units of different sizes: miles are good for measuring the distance between two cities, inches are good for measuring a cake, and yards for measuring a racetrack. As they are all units of length or distance, we can mix them together—so a child can be 4 feet 9 inches tall.

The Burj Khalifa in Dubai, UAE, is 2,723 feet tall—more than half a mile!

TECH TIME

A laser meter measures distances very precisely by bouncing a laser beam off the wall. It works by timing how long it takes for the reflected beam to come back—it's much more accurate than a tape measure! NASA bounces laser beams off a mirror placed on the surface of the moon by the Apollo missions to measure the distance to the moon. They've discovered that the moon is drifting farther away by 1.5 inches a year!

Measuring up

Near enough

Sometimes precision matters. A dentist measuring your teeth for braces measures really accurately and precisely. Someone measuring you for a costume for a school play only needs to be right to within an inch or so. They can round to the nearest inch.

The landing place for Perseverance was chosen precisely—rounding the distance could have landed it uselessly in a crater.

Rounding helps you make approximations and rough calculations, and makes something easy to read or understand. NASA reported the voyage of the rover Perseverance to Mars as taking about seven months and covering about 300 million miles. This would be good enough for you to do a school project on Perseverance, but NASA had to know exactly how far the craft was going to travel or it might miss Mars entirely!

As well as choosing suitable *units*, you need to choose a suitable level of precision. You might need to "round" your measurement. ***Rounding*** is giving a number close to the precise answer, but "rounded up" or "rounded down" to the nearest whole number, for example 10, 100, or 1,000. Rounding can be useful in lots of circumstances—but not all!

In sports, time is often measured to thousandths of a second so world records are set with astonishing precision. The Suzuka Formula One racing circuit in Japan is 3.608 miles long. The record holder completed a lap in 1 minute 30.965 seconds, and the record could be beaten if someone was a thousandth of a second faster! But if you planned to watch a race, you would only need to know about how long it was going to last.

DID YOU KNOW?

Your weight varies by a few ounces during a day, so if you weigh yourself too precisely it's soon wrong. Even more surprisingly, your height changes, too. You are tallest in the morning, when you have been lying down all night. After a day being upright, gravity squashes your vertebrae down a bit, making you slightly shorter!

You stretch while you sleep!

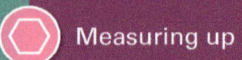 Measuring up

Quick change

Imagine you start watching a movie that's 143 minutes long two-and-a-half hours before it's time for bed. Can you watch to the end? To find out how many hours the film lasts, divide 143 by 60 because there are 60 minutes in an hour: 143 ÷ 60 = 2.38 hours.

But you want the answer in hours and minutes. Two hours is 2 × 60 = 120 minutes. Subtracting this from 143 leaves 23 minutes. The film lasts 2 hours and 23 minutes—you can see it all!

When you measure things, you might need to switch between *units*, for example changing ounces to pounds, or days to weeks. That involves dividing and multiplying, sometimes by unusual numbers.

You might sometimes need to convert between inches and feet (12 inches to the foot), feet and yards (3 feet to the yard), or yards and miles (1,760 yards to the mile).

We can also use different types of units together. We measure speed in miles per hour—how far something travels in an hour tells us how fast it's going. Some sound strange: a foot-candle is the light falling on a surface held 1 foot from a regular candle. It's used to measure lighting in the movie industry, and in galleries and museums.

In summer, water falls over Niagara Falls, Canada, at the rate of 100,000 cubic feet per second.

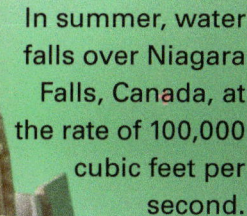

CURIOUS CONNECTIONS

PHYSICS Scientists often need to measure pushes, pulls, and other movements. They measure pressure as weight pushing on an area, such as pounds per square inch. They can measure water flow as *volume* moving through time, such as gallons per second. That can tell you how long it takes to fill a swimming pool.

ALL AREAS

When you compare the sizes of two pizzas, or decide whether you and your friends can fit into a small tent, you're really working with areas. Area crops up in all kinds of places when you're not thinking about it! If you buy fabric to make a Halloween costume, or roll out pastry to cover a pie, you are making sure you have a large enough area of fabric or pastry for your task.

If my calculations are correct, this field is the perfect size!

How do you work out which size pizza to buy? Can you tell whether a field is big enough to play baseball? Can you fit three sleeping bags on the floor of that tent? These are questions about area. Area is the space taken up by a flat shape.

A superhero needs the right area of fabric for a good cape!

Even three-dimensional objects have an area—it's the area of the surface. You have a *surface area*! Your area is smaller than that of an adult, which is why your clothes are probably smaller than your parents' clothes. And a room has an area of walls, ceiling, and floor. That's an area on the inside, not the outside!

It takes more shampoo to wash a big dog than a small dog because the big dog has a larger surface area.

 All areas

Flat out

Think of a flowerbed in a garden or park. If the flowerbed is rectangular, its area is its width times its length. If you measure it in feet, the area is in square feet.

This flowerbed is 4 feet long by 2 feet wide, so its area is 2 × 4 = 8 square feet.

Areas don't have to be square to be measured in square units, though. You could take a piece of paper of one square inch, cut it up and rearrange it as a triangle and it would still have an area of one square inch. And you can cut up a rectangle and rearrange the parts—even if some have been cut into triangles—and the area will still be the same.

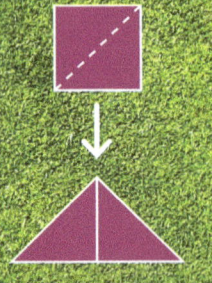

You can figure out the area of any shape by calculating how many squares of a set size it covers.

We usually measure area in "square" *units*, such as square feet, square inches, or square miles. One square inch is the area covered by a square that has sides one inch long.

The area of Iceland is 39,817 square miles—but the country is far from square!

Even a shape with a really complicated or wiggly *perimeter* (outline) still has an area measured in square units. Most countries have very complicated shapes, but we can compare their sizes by stating their areas in square miles.

TECH TIME

Solar panels generate electricity from sunlight falling on them. The larger the area of the solar panel, the more electricity is produced. Solar panels are angled so that they get the most possible sunlight and none of the surface is in shade. We can measure their output in kilowatt hours per square meter or square foot.

 All areas

Re-do your room

Most rooms have rectangular walls with rectangular doors and windows. To find the area of a rectangle, you multiply the length of the long side by the length of the short side.

Walls: $10 \times 8 = 80 \quad \times 2 = 160$
$15 \times 8 = 120 \quad \times 2 = \underline{+240}$
$400 \ ft^2$
Ceiling: $10 \times 15 = 150 \ ft^2$
Window: $5 \times 3 = 15 \ ft^2$
Door: $3 \times 7 = 21 \ ft^2$

Total area: $400 + 150 - 15 - 21 = 514 \ ft^2$
Two coats: $514 \times 2 = 1028 \ ft^2$

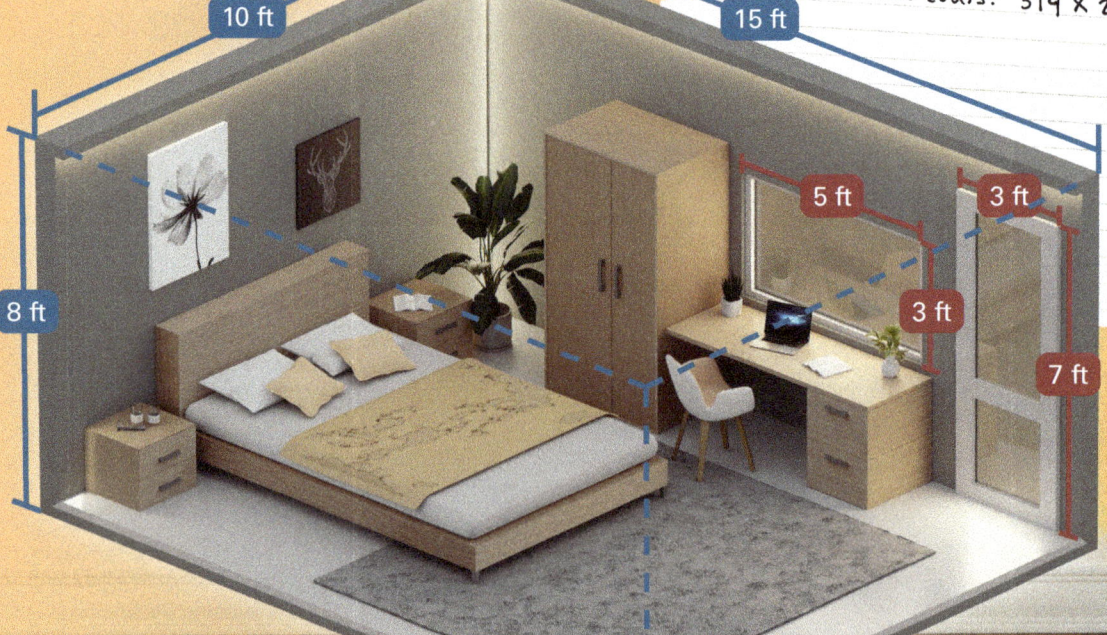

For a square, all sides are the same so you can just multiply the side by itself. Multiplying a number by itself is called squaring it, because it's what you do when you find the area of a square!

Is your room looking a little tired? How about a coat of paint to brighten it up! First, you will need to know how much paint to buy. You have to start by figuring out the area of the walls you want to paint.

The label on a paint can shows the area in square feet that you can cover with that can. First, measure all the walls and work out their areas. Don't forget the ceiling, if you're painting that! Then measure the doors and windows and subtract their areas. Add up the areas to be painted. You will usually need two coats of paint, so double the area.

To figure out how much paint you need, you'll have to divide the area you're going to paint by how much one can will cover. If you need to paint 600 square feet and a can covers 350 square feet, you will need two cans—you can't buy a part of a can.

CAREER CORNER

Interior designers help people to design their living space, and even the spaces of office buildings and hotels. They are experts on combining colors, textures, and different materials. Their work is creative and artistic, but they need a good grasp of math to work out the materials needed and the costs.

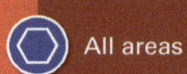 All areas

More pizza?

Suppose you want to buy pizza for eight people. If you can eat an 8-inch pizza on your own, should you buy four 16-inch pizzas? Not unless you are all very hungry!

You can measure the amount of pizza you eat by area. The area of a circle is calculated from the *radius*—half the distance across the middle of the pizza. The area of a circle is radius × radius × π (called *pi*). Pi is a special number, approximately 3.14, used in math to work with circles. In fact, pi goes on and on forever with more numbers after the decimal point. Mathematicians call numbers like this *irrational numbers*. In this book, we will round all our answers to two digits after the decimal point.

Math is delicious!

After all that painting, you'll be hungry!

How about a pizza? But how much should you buy? Pizzas come in many sizes, and it's not always easy to know which one to order. You can use math to choose which size pizza you need.

An 8-inch pizza has a radius of ½ × 8 = 4 inches. That means the area of an 8-inch pizza is about 4 × 4 × 3.14 = 50.24 square inches.

The area of a 16-inch pizza is about 8 × 8 × 3.14 = 200.96 square inches. That is four times the size of the smaller pizza! When the radius doubles, the area quadruples.

CURIOUS CONNECTIONS

ASTRONOMY Space scientists use π in calculations to work out the size of planets—it's useful for working with spheres as well as flat circles. From measuring distance across a planet, they can work out the whole area of its surface.

3 IN PROPORTION

Mathematicians talk about proportions using *ratios*. A ratio shows how big one quantity or dimension (measurement) is compared to another.

The ratio of white chickens to brown chickens is 3:2

Have you ever accidentally ruined one of your pictures by messing up the proportions? Maybe you drew a head that was far too small for the body. Or maybe you resized your image on the computer and made it too wide or too tall, distorting the picture.

The ratio of coffee to milk marks the difference between different types of drink

We can use ratios to compare numbers in lots of different settings.
In a class of 30 children, if 15 had a dog and five had a cat, the ratio of dogs to cats would be 15:5. Because 15 ÷ 5 = 3, we can simplify the ratio from 15:5 to 3:1. You probably use ratios a lot already without even realizing it. If you are drawing a picture, you try to get the proportions of the body right—the legs longer than the arms, the head smaller than the body—even if you don't know the exact ratio. Let's see where they turn up in everyday life.

People have used ratios for thousands of years. The first person to write about them was the Greek mathematician **Euclid**, around 2,300 years ago. Euclid wrote a famous book called *Elements* that explained *geometry* (the math of shapes), proved some mathematical ideas, and set out basic statements that can be taken as true in math. His work was important for more than 2,000 years.

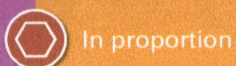
In proportion

All the same

If your picture is 6 inches wide and 10 inches tall and you double the width, you need to double the height. Ratios are all about simple multiplication and division. Imagine you and three friends have been given 20 strawberries. That's clearly five strawberries each because 20 ÷ 4 = 5. You can say the ratio of strawberries to people is 5:1 (five strawberries for one person)—or the ratio of people to strawberries is 1:5 (one person to five strawberries).

CURIOUS CONNECTIONS

ART Artists know the right proportions for different parts of the human body and use that math knowledge to make sure their drawings and paintings look realistic. But the proportions change as we grow! A baby's head is a larger proportion of its body than an adult's. A one-year-old has a body:head ratio of 4:1, but for an adult the ratio is 9:1.

Often, we need *ratios* to stay the same.
If you resize your picture, you want all sides to change by the same multiple, so the picture stays in proportion. If you make it twice as wide, you want it to be twice as tall.

The ratio between the two sides of a picture is called the "aspect ratio". It's important to keep it the same when you resize a picture.

To help you figure out ratios, you can draw up a ratio table. It has two columns, one for each side of the ratio. In each row, the first number is multiplied by the same factor to get the second number.

You could use this ratio table to work out your weight on Jupiter! Because Jupiter has stronger gravity than Earth, you weigh 2.5 times as much on Jupiter.

Weight on Earth	Weight on Jupiter
60 lb	150 lb
80 lb	200 lb
100 lb	250 lb
120 lb	300 lb

The ratio is 1:2.5, which we usually write as 2:5 because we use whole numbers.

25

In proportion

Lemonade stand

All recipes work on the basis of the proportions of different ingredients. Although they tell you precise quantities, such as 2 cups of flour and 1 cup of sugar, it's the ratios that are important: twice as much flour as sugar, in this case.

You don't have to stick to the same *units* as the original recipe, but you do need to use the same type of measure. Instead of cups, you could use another measure of *volume*, such as pints, or even buckets! But you can't swap from volume to weight.

Change the quantities of ingredients to make more or less of a recipe. Just keep the ratios the same or the recipe won't work.

CAREER CORNER

A pharmacist provides people with medicines. They sometimes have to figure out the dose depending on age of a child or weight of an adult. Age is related to size—children grow larger as they get older. The pharmacist uses ratios to work out doses, often as milligrams per kilogram of body weight.

Do you like cooking? If so, you will already be using *ratios* without even realizing it.

Most recipes have more than two ingredients, so you have a three- or four-way ratio. They work in just the same way.

A recipe for lemonade might use a cup of sugar, 8 lemons and 32 fluid ounces of water. The ratio of sugar to lemons to water is 1:8:32. You could make any quantity of lemonade using these proportions. Here's a ratio table to help:

	Sugar (cups)	Lemons	Water (fl oz)
Original Recipe	1	8	32
Double quantity, × 2	2	16	64
Treble quantity, × 3	3	24	96
Half quantity, × ½	½	4	16

What if you only had six lemons? This is three-quarters the number of lemons. How much sugar and water do you think you would need?

 In proportion

Plots and **plans**

Architects design buildings— everything from houses to airports and factories. They make scale models and plans of the project so that people can see what it will look like and can figure out the materials needed. Computer-based scale models even let you "walk" through the building on screen.

Town planning involves working at different scales: small scales for maps of a whole town, larger scales for a small district and even larger scales for individual buildings.

Have you ever made a model from a kit, or following plans in a book or online? Models use the same proportions as a full-size object, but at a different scale. A model plane will be smaller than the real thing, while a drawing of an insect is larger. Plots, plans, and maps are all drawings made to scale.

All the parts of a model plane are made to scale so they fit together and the finished model looks just like the real plane, but smaller.

In a scale drawing or model, all the dimensions are changed by the same factor. They might be twice as big as the original size, or a hundredth the original size, for example. The scale is expressed as a *ratio*. An interior designer might draw a plan of a single room using a scale of 1:20. That means 1 inch on the plan represents 20 inches in the room. The scale is not specific to one unit. If 1 inch shows 20 inches, 1 centimeter shows 20 centimeters, and 1 foot shows 20 feet.

CAREER CORNER

Cartographers draw maps, which are scale plans of an area of land—it can even be land on another planet or the moon! Long ago, land was surveyed and maps drawn by hand, but modern cartographers can take data from satellite images and measurements and use computers to help them. Maps are drawn to scales such as 1:10,000 because they must be much smaller than the land they show.

Some cartographers even map other planets! This map of Mercury was made from measurements made by a spacecraft flying around the planet.

4 SAVE OR SPEND?

You will spend a lot of your adult life earning and managing money, so it's good to get a head start and build your confidence. Billionaires don't just happen!

Use addition and subtraction to work out what you're spending and how much change to expect

How long would it take you to save for a guitar, a hat, or a book you want? How much will you have if you save your allowance or earnings for five weeks? What if you put it in a savings account—how much extra would you get?

Not all coins are round! Some ancient Chinese money was shaped like knives or spades.

Long ago, people didn't use money as we think of it. Instead, they used such objects as shells, or items that had genuine useful value, such as grain you could eat, or tools you could use. The first metal coins appeared about **2,500 years** ago in China, Greece, and India.

Lots of clever people spend their time figuring out how to get you to spend your money on the things they sell, but you don't have to fall for it. With a bit of your own thinking you can hunt for good deals, or make your money grow.

Let's take a look at how you can out-smart stores to make your money go further.

31

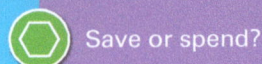

Save or spend?

Buy, buy, buy

Some stores offer such deals as "buy one, get one half price", "three for the price of two", or "one third off". It's not always easy to see which you should go for.

Imagine three bookstores are having a sale on books by your favorite author. The books are usually $10 each.

You pay $10 + $5 = $15 for two books. That's $7.50 for each book.

BUY 1, GET 1 HALF PRICE!

You pay $10 + $10 = $20 for three books. That's $10 ÷ 3 = $6.66 for each book—but you have to buy three.

3 for the price of 2 on ALL BOOKS!

You pay $10 − $3.33 = $6.67 for each book. This looks good!

ONE THIRD OFF ANY BOOK!

When you go shopping, you need to keep your eyes open and your wits sharp to get the best deal. Stores come up with lots of special offers to try to persuade you to part with your money. If you know your math, you can work out which deals are good for you, and which are not so good.

How do these offers pan out?

Unless you really want three books, the first deal is the worst, even though it looks quite enticing. The last deal is best, as you can buy just one book and still get the savings. "Buy one get one half price" looks good, but you're paying more per book—and you have to buy two.

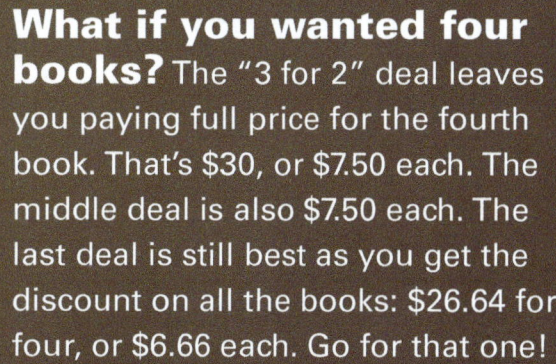

What if you wanted four books? The "3 for 2" deal leaves you paying full price for the fourth book. That's $30, or $7.50 each. The middle deal is also $7.50 each. The last deal is still best as you get the discount on all the books: $26.64 for four, or $6.66 each. Go for that one!

Save or spend?

One in a hundred

Sale prices are often shown as a percentage off the full price—a reduction of 10%, 15% or 20%, for example. Each percentage point is one hundredth of the price. If an item is $100, one percent of its cost is $1. If each item is $50, one percent is 50 cents. Suppose a computer game originally cost $50, but is advertised with 20% off. Because 1% is 50 cents, 20% would be 20 × 50 = 1,000 cents, or $10. Subtract the discount to find out what you have to pay: $50 − $10 = $40.

You have to do a bit of math to make the most of the sales. Imagine you see a T-shirt you like that was $25, but is now 25% off. You have $20; can you afford it? Let's see: 1% of $25 is 25 cents. With 25% off, you will save 25 × 25 cents = 625 cents, or $6.25. As $25 − $6.25 = $18.75, you can afford it—a successful shopping trip!

Lots of stores have cut-price sales. They move old stock out of the way for new items, or they reduce prices in events like Black Friday sales. How much can you really save?

In Russia, the population of Amur tigers has increased by 15 percent in ten years, from around 470 to 540.

You see percentages in places other than stores. News articles might tell you that 10% of people are vegetarian, or 60% of people watch a particular TV show.

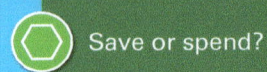 Save or spend?

A lot of **interest**

Imagine you get $100 for your birthday and put it in a savings account. If the bank pays you 5% interest each year, after one year you will have your original $100 and 5% interest, which is an extra $5—a total of $105. The next year you will get 5% of $105, so then you will have $105 + $5.25 = $110.25.

If you need to borrow money (perhaps when you're older!), you have to pay the bank interest. If you borrow $100 at 10% interest, after one year you would owe $110—the original $100 and $10 in interest.

Buying a house is very expensive because you have to pay interest on the loan. Borrowing $400,000 at 5% interest costs 5 × $4,000 = $20,000 a year just in interest.

Don't spend all your money in the sales!
If you save it in a bank account, you will get extra—the bank pays you a percentage of your money each year as *interest*.

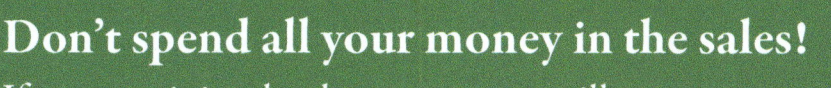

While your savings grow, prices might go up. This is called *inflation*. If prices rise 10%, a hat that cost $10 last year might cost $11 this year. Inflation means you can buy less with the same money. If you had $20 last year, you could buy two hats, but this year you can only buy one, with just $9 left over.

DID YOU KNOW?

Percentages can get out of hand! In Hungary, after World War II (1939–1945), prices rose by 12,950,000,000,000,000 percent in a month, which meant they doubled every 15 hours. This is called "hyperinflation" and causes catastrophe for a country.

5

IN THE CENTER

A question like "What is the temperature in Florida in July?" can't be answered precisely because the temperature varies. We can give a range, which is the highest and lowest temperatures. Or we can calculate a typical temperature by recording the temperature each day in July and figuring out a central figure. Mathematicians have three ways of measuring the center figure in a group of numbers.

A star rating for a product is the mean: all the ratings are added together, and the total is divided by the number of ratings.

You won't need a warm coat in June!

4.3 ★★★★★ 111 ratings

How do you know whether to take a warm coat or a swimsuit when you go on vacation? You probably check what the temperature is likely to be in the resort for the month you're going. This won't predict the exact temperatures for your vacation, but it tells you what to expect.

The *median* is the value in the middle of a range.

In terms of size, the white egg is the median.

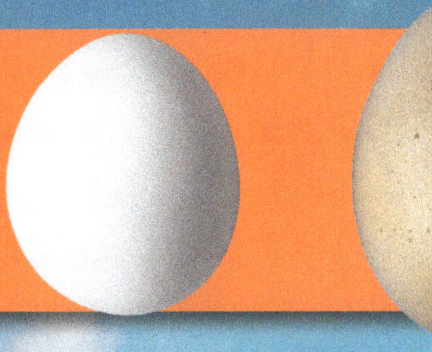

The *mode* is the figure that turns up most often in the data.

C is the mode on this answer sheet because it's chosen most often.

The *mean* is calculated by adding up the figures and dividing by the number of values. When people say "average" in everyday conversation, they usually intend the mean.

The mean temperature in Florida in July is 82 °F. That's useful info if you are planning to visit.

Read on to find out how useful the mean, mode, and median can be in your life.

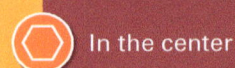 In the center

Know what to **expect**

Mean

We calculate the mean by counting the candies in several bags, adding up the total, and dividing by the number of bags.

These five bags contain 405 candies all together, so the mean contents is 405 ÷ 5 = 81.

Mode

The *mode* is the number that occurs most often. Two of these bags have 81 candies, so the mode is 81. There would be no mode if all the bags had a different number of candies.

A skating rink needs to know which size of skates is needed most often—the mode.

Golf players are given a handicap to even out their abilities. The handicap is figured out using the mean of a player's 8 best scores out of their 20 most recent scores.

You might have bought a bag of candy sold by weight that tells you the "average contents." For a mathematician, it's the *mean*. It lets you know roughly how many candies you can expect to find in the bag. The mean is the contents of a typical bag, but any single bag might contain more or fewer candies.

Median

The range of numbers of candies in this example is 79 to 84. If we put the bags in order of size, we see that the figure in the middle is 81; this is the *median*.

With an even number of values, there are two figures in the middle. The median is then halfway between them. Here it's 80.5:

Two children are taller and two shorter than the median.

In the center

On trend

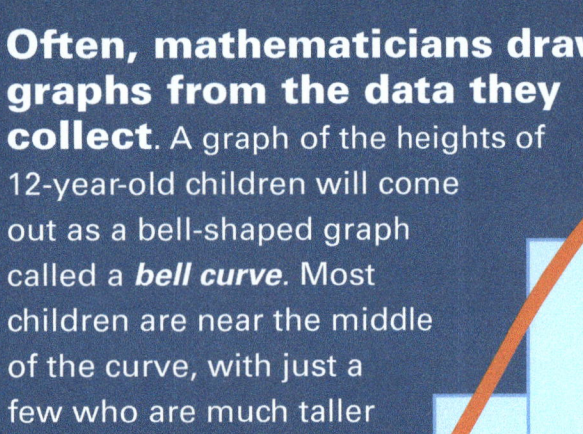

"My height is average!"

Often, mathematicians draw graphs from the data they collect. A graph of the heights of 12-year-old children will come out as a bell-shaped graph called a **bell curve**. Most children are near the middle of the curve, with just a few who are much taller or shorter.

A teacher looks at your grades to make sure you're making the expected progress for your age

This type of graph is useful for showing trends, and for spotting if something is unusual and needs attention. If someone's height was right at the bottom of the range (the left of the graph), they might need a medical check. If a student's grades were at the far right of the curve, they might be given enrichment tasks to challenge them. Comparing with central figures is a good way of checking someone's progress, but it's only a guide—we are all different.

Different types of average can help us check progress and make predictions, such as which sports teams might excel, what sizes children will be at different ages, and how much rain falls in different places.

Knowing what is usual is vital if we are to spot what's unusual. Tracking the temperature over decades means we can see the mean global temperature is rising. Recording from year to year when birds migrate or flowers appear lets us identify any changes in the pattern.

As the climate changes, the *mean* times birds migrate shift.

If someone's temperature is too far from the mean, medical staff will look for signs of illness.

Activity

In this activity, you will make a scale drawing of your room and the furniture in it, or of a room you would love to have if you could. You will draw everything with the same proportions as the real objects have and then move the items around on your room plan to find the perfect arrangement.

You will need:

- Measuring tape or yardstick
- Paper
- Pencil
- Ruler
- Eraser
- Scissors
- Colored pencils if you want to bring your design to life!

Give it a try

1. Start by choosing a scale—such as one inch representing one foot (12 inches). This scale is 1:12. If your room is 10 feet long, you will draw a plan 10 inches long. If your room is 20 feet long, you might want to use a smaller scale, such as 1:24 (half an inch to one foot) to keep your plan a manageable size.

2. Draw up a ratio table to help you convert your measurements using the scale you've chosen. If you were using 1:12, for example, your table would start like this:

1	12
2	24
3	36
4	48
5	60

3. Measure the lengths of all the walls and draw the outline of your room to scale on your plan.

Could your room do with a make-over? It's heavy work shifting furniture around, and it's annoying if you move things and find they don't fit. There's a better way to try out new arrangements—or even a new fantasy room!

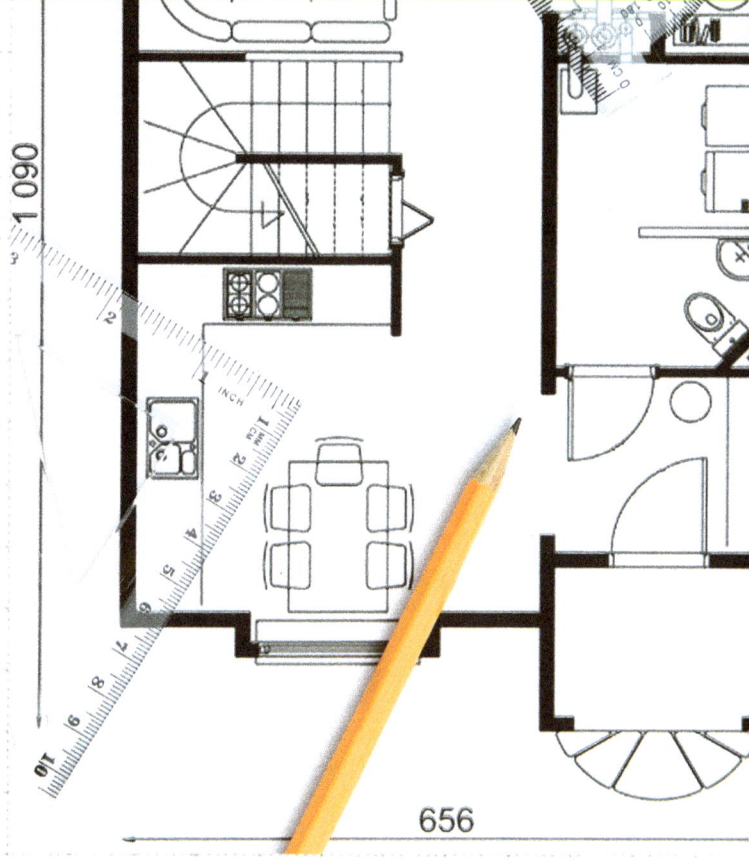

4. Measure the doors, windows, heaters, and anything else you can't move and mark them on your plan to scale at exactly the right positions. Measure how far the door is from the corner, for example, so you can draw it in the right place.

5. Measure each piece of furniture in your room. Draw little paper shapes of each, using the same scale as you use for the room, and cut them out. If your bed is 6 feet long by 3 feet wide, and your scale is 1:12, draw a rectangle 6 inches by 3 inches. You can add color and patterns to your bits of furniture—maybe a bright new comforter?

6. Now you can move the little paper furniture around to see how well it fits in different arrangements. Don't forget you need to leave room to open closet doors and drawers and to get in and out of bed!

Try this next!

Now that you know how to draw rooms to scale, challenge yourself to design your dream house. What rooms will you include? What will you place in those rooms? Make sure your proportions and sizes make sense!

QUESTION TIME!

What scale did you choose to use? Why did you choose this scale instead of something different?

Index

A
Amur tigers, 35
architecture, 28
area, 13-21
art, 24
aspect ratios, 25
astronomy, 21
automobile racing, 11
average, 39, 41, 43

B
bird migration, 43
Burj Khalifa, 9

C
cartography, 29
circles, 20-21
cubic feet, 13

D
division, 12-13, 19, 24, 38-40

E
Euclid, 23

F
feet, 8-9, 13, 16-17, 19, 29, 44-45
foot-candles, 13

G
germs, 7
graphs, 42
gravity, 11, 25

H
hours, 12-13
hyperinflation, 37

I
Iceland, 17
inches, 8-10, 13, 16, 21, 29, 44
interest (finance), 36-37
interior design, 19, 29
irrational numbers, 20

J
Jupiter, 25

K
kilograms, 6, 26
kilowatt hours, 17

L
lasers, 9

M
maps, 28-29
Mars, 10
mean, 38-41, 43

median, 39, 41
Mercury, 29
miles, 8-11, 13, 16-17
miles per hour, 13
minutes, 6, 11-12
mode, 39-40
models, 28-29
moon, of Earth, 9, 29
multiplication, 12-13, 18, 24-25

N
nanometers, 7
National Aeronautics and Space Administration (NASA), 9-10
Niagara Falls, 13

O
ounces, 11, 27

P
percentages, 34-37
Perseverance (rover), 10
pharmacist (career), 26
physics, 13
pi, 20
pints, 6, 26
pounds, 6, 13
precision, 10-11
proportions, 22-29, 44-45

R
radius, 20-21
ratios, 22-27, 29, 44
recipes, 26-27

S
sale prices, 34-35
scale drawings, 29, 44-45
scale models, 28-29
shopping deals, 32-33
solar panels, 17
sports, 11, 43
square feet, 16-17, 19
square inches, 13, 16, 21
square miles, 16-17
surface area, 15
switching between units, 12-13

T
temperature ranges, 38-39, 43
town planning, 28

Y
yards, 8-9, 13

Glossary

bell curve (behl kurv)—the normal distribution of a set of measurements

cartographer (kahr TOG ruh fuhr)—a person who creates maps

geometry (jee OM uh tree)—the math of shapes

hands (handz)—the unit of measurement used for measuring the height of horses

inflation (ihn FLAY shuhn)—the way prices for goods and services increase over time

interest (IHN tuhr ihst)—a small percentage of money paid by the bank for keeping money in your account or charged to a person for borrowing money

irrational numbers (ih RASH uh nuhl NUHM buhrz—numbers that cannot be expressed as a simple fraction, and their decimal goes on forever without repeating

mean (meen)—the sum of the data divided by the number of data values

median (MEE dee uhn)—the value in the middle when the data is listed from least to greatest

mode (mohd)—the most common value in a data set

nanometer (NAN-oh-MEE-ter)—a unit of measurement that is one billionth of a meter

perimeter (puh RIHM uh tuhr)—the outline or boundary of a shape

pi (py)—the ratio of a circle's circumference to its diameter, approximately 3.14

radius (RAY dee uhs)—the distance from the center of a circle to any point on its circumference

ratio (RAY shee oh)—a comparison that indicates how big or small something is compared to another

rounding (ROWN dihng)—a rough calculation of an answer that is not precise

solar panels (SOH luhr PAN uhlz)—devices that convert sunlight into electricity

surface area (SUR fihs AIR ee uh)—the measure of total area taken up by the sides of a three-dimensional shape

units (YOO nihtz)—standard measurements used to express the quantity of something

volume (VOL yuhm)—a measurement of capacity, or how much space a three-dimensional object takes up

www.ingramcontent.com/pod-product-compliance
Lightning Source LLC
Chambersburg PA
CBHW061252170426
43191CB00041B/2414